ESSAYS IN INTERNATIONAL FINANCE

No. 164, September 1986

DISASTER MYOPIA
IN INTERNATIONAL BANKING

JACK M. GUTTENTAG

AND

RICHARD J. HERRING

INTERNATIONAL FINANCE SECTION

DEPARTMENT OF ECONOMICS
PRINCETON UNIVERSITY
PRINCETON, NEW JERSEY

INTERNATIONAL FINANCE SECTION
EDITORIAL STAFF

Peter B. Kenen, *Director*
Ellen Seiler, *Editor*
Carolyn Kappes, *Editorial Aide*
Barbara Radvany, *Subscriptions and Orders*

Library of Congress Cataloging-in-Publication Data

Guttentag, Jack M., 1923
  Disaster myopia in international banking.

  (Essays in international finance, ISSN 0071-142X ; no. 164)
  Bibliography: p.
  1. Banks and banking, International.   2. International finance.   I. Herring,
Richard.   II. Title.   III. Series. HG136.P7   no. 164   [HG3881]   332'.042 s
86-15258
ISBN 0-88165-071-4   [332.1'5]

Printed in the United States of America by Princeton University Press at Princeton, New Jersey.

ISSN: 0071-142X
ISBN: 0-88165-071-4
LC Catalog Card Number: 86-15258

CONTENTS

DISASTER MYOPIA IN INTERNATIONAL BANKING

This essay explores the hypothesis that international banks tend to assume excessive exposure to insolvency. It builds on a framework developed in an earlier paper (Guttentag and Herring, 1984) that shows why the financial system tends to become increasingly vulnerable to major shocks during long periods when no such shocks occur. The focus in this essay on a particular sector of the financial system is not only a compelling illustration of the general thesis but also of interest in its own right because international banking has assumed strategic importance in the financial disorders of the 1980s.

Section 1 sets out the basic conceptual framework and explains the conditions conducive to disaster myopia. Section 2 examines the exposure of international banks to major transfer shocks, and section 3 examines their exposure to funding shocks. Section 4 assesses the ability of regulators to prevent an increase in vulnerability to both types of shocks.

1 Conceptual Framework

Risk and Uncertainty

We follow a venerable and useful tradition in economics, extending from J. M. Keynes and F. H. Knight, that distinguishes risk from uncertainty. Suppose p_i is the probability that the ith event will occur. Pure uncertainty describes the situation where we know nothing about the size of p_i. Pure risk describes the situation where p_i takes on a value between zero and one that is known with complete confidence. (Perfect certainty describes the situation where we know that p_i is either zero or one. Note that our usage differs from one commonly employed in the modern literature on finance, where risk is the dispersion of possible outcomes around the expected outcome.)

With regard to most events, our knowledge is intermediate between pure uncertainty and pure risk. We do not know p_i, but we have some evidence that allows us to estimate it. The greater our confidence in that estimate, the closer we approach the case of pure risk. The lower our confidence, the closer we approach the case of pure uncertainty.

Two major factors determine the extent to which our knowledge about an event is characterized by risk or uncertainty. The first is the frequency with

Research for this essay has been supported by a grant from the National Science Foundation to the Brookings Institution for an experimental program of research on issues of international economic policy. The views expressed here should not be attributed to the officers, trustees, or other staff members of the Brookings Institution. The authors are grateful to an anonymous referee for helpful comments on an earlier draft.

1

which the event occurs relative to the frequency of changes in the underlying causal structure. If that structure changes every time an event occurs, the events do not generate evidence regarding probabilities. If the event occurs many times but the structure is stable, we accumulate evidence that permits us to estimate probabilities with considerable confidence. For example, if floods over a plain occur on average only once in every twenty-five years but basic topographic and climatic conditions are stable, an historical record over several hundred years may yield good estimates of flood probabilities. Despite the low probability of a flood in any short period, our knowledge about the probability of a flood is closer to pure risk than to uncertainty. In contrast, the causal structure underlying economic developments is unlikely to remain stable for long periods, so that it is very difficult to estimate the probability of low-frequency economic events with much confidence. Our knowledge about their probability is much closer to uncertainty.

The second factor that determines whether a situation is better characterized by risk or uncertainty is our understanding of the underlying causal structure. The probability that the fair toss of a coin will generate heads is an example of pure risk, because our prior knowledge of the mechanism determining the result allows us to specify its exact probability, even if we have no knowledge of the results of prior tosses. In contrast, our understanding of the causal structures underlying economic processes is much less comprehensive and therefore much more likely to be subject to uncertainty.

Sometimes the probability of an event can be estimated with greater confidence by investing in information and analysis. This conversion of uncertainty into risk is the central objective of the risk analysis that takes place in most financial institutions.

Shocks and Insolvency Exposure

"Shocks" are events that occur very infrequently and have very large potential effects. Since our understanding of the causal structure underlying economic shocks is imperfect and since the causal structure may change between occurrences, our knowledge regarding economic shocks is closer to the case of pure uncertainty than pure risk.

Financial institutions engage in a variety of activities exposing them to such shocks. The shocks include defaults by a major category of borrowers ("credit shocks") and runs by depositors ("funding shocks"). Any shock that would reduce an institution's net worth is a source of insolvency exposure. An institution's insolvency exposure becomes "excessive" when its exposure-management policies have been based on underestimates of shock probabilities. "Disaster myopia" is a systematic tendency to underestimate shock probabilities.

2

The Disaster-Myopia Hypothesis

Under conditions of uncertainty, there can be no presumption that the subjective probabilities that market participants attach to a shock will converge to the actual probabilities. The argument that market discipline will require decisionmakers to form correct expectations has little force: the shock may occur so infrequently that institutions which disregard it completely may survive for decades. Indeed, competition may drive prudent institutions from the market. An institution that attempts to charge an appropriate premium to develop a reserve against a low-probability shock is likely to lose business to competitors who are willing to disregard the shock.

How are subjective shock probabilities formulated? Economic theory offers little guidance. As Lucas (1977) has observed, the rational-expectations hypothesis and efficient-market axioms simply do not apply in situations of uncertainty. Our hypothesis is drawn instead from work on cognitive psychology and the behavioral approach to decisionmaking under uncertainty. We believe that two of the "heuristics" that have been found to characterize human behavior with regard to low-probability, high-loss hazards provide insights into the behavior of international banks confronted with shocks of low but unknown probability.

The "availability heuristic" is a term employed by Tversky and Kahneman (1982, p. 164) to describe situations in which the decisionmaker "estimates frequency or probability by the ease with which instances or association can be brought to mind." Its validity has been verified in both controlled laboratory experiments and field work.[1] Frequent events are usually easier to recall than infrequent events. But ease of recall is affected by other factors that may have little or no relationship to probabilities, giving rise to an availability bias. One such factor is the time elapsed since the last occurrence.

The "threshold heuristic" is an implicit rule by which decisionmakers allocate one of their scarcest resources, managerial attention, and it may also contribute to bias. The rule is that when a probability reaches some critically low level, it is treated as if it were zero.[2]

---

[1] Tversky and Kahneman (1982) report results of ten controlled experiments performed with 1,500 subjects which demonstrated that even when probabilities could be objectively determined, people tended to employ the availability heuristic. The authors argue that their results are equally applicable to very infrequent events where probability judgments cannot be based on a tally of relative frequencies. Kunreuther *et al.* (1978) conclude from a field survey of 2,000 homeowners in flood-prone areas and 1,000 homeowners in earthquake-prone areas that insurance decisions with regard to low-probability, high-loss hazards are subject to the availability bias.

[2] The threshold heuristic is based on the work of Herbert Simon concerning procedural rationality (see Simon, 1978, for a recent overview). Slovic *et al.* (1977) employed the hypothesis to

The availability heuristic in combination with the threshold heuristic may lead to disaster myopia, which can be defined as a tendency to underestimate shock probabilities. The subjective probability of a shock becomes a negative function of the length of time since the last shock and at some point is treated as if it were zero.[3] Disaster myopia leads decisionmakers to allow the shock exposure of their firms to rise and the ability of their firms to withstand shocks to decline. In consequence, insolvency exposure grows as the period since the last shock lengthens. If this pattern is widespread among firms, the entire system becomes more vulnerable to shocks and to a possible financial crisis (see Guttentag and Herring, 1984, for a further discussion of the evolution of the conditions leading to a financial crisis).

There are epistemological limitations to use of the disaster-myopia hypothesis as an explanation of insolvency exposure, and to use of the availability and threshold heuristics as explanations for disaster myopia itself. It is impossible to demonstrate *ex ante* excessive insolvency exposure to shocks of unknown probability. Indeed, it is impossible even after a shock has occurred. If excessive insolvency exposure is nondemonstrable, disaster myopia, which is only one of the possible causes of excessive insolvency exposure, is also nondemonstrable.

Nevertheless, valid judgments on both topics can be made, even though they will be inconclusive. Many diseases have been known by their symptoms, and sometimes by the conditions associated with the symptoms, well before the pathogenic substance could be identified by a definitive diagnostic test. While a definitive test for disaster myopia is probably impossible, we know many of its symptoms and the conditions that encourage it. For example, a lack of information about shock exposures is a good indication that no thought has been given to the probability that a shock will occur. From a policy standpoint, however, it is less important to recognize the symptoms of disaster myopia than to understand the conditions that encourage it.

Conditions Conducive to Disaster Myopia

Disaster myopia is a perceptual bias that we have associated with two heuristics commonly used to deal with uncertainty. This perceptual bias will lead to excessive insolvency exposure if toleration of exposure to potential shocks appears profitable. Given disaster myopia, the incentive to increase insolvency

---

explain why people may refuse to buy insurance against low-probability hazards. Kunreuther *et al.* (1978) find evidence supporting the threshold heuristic in their field survey of the insurance decisions of 3,000 households.

[3] When the interval between shocks is very long, the Bayesian approach to decisionmaking leads to the same behavior as the availability heuristic, i.e., the subjective probability of a shock declines with the passage of time since the last such shock and at some point reaches zero (see Guttentag and Herring, 1984).

4

exposure rises with the anticipated returns (net of underestimated required loss reserves).

To some degree, uncertainty can be converted into risk through investment in information. Information confronts disaster myopia with contrary evidence that may correct it. But the conditions that encourage disaster myopia also reduce the willingness of firms to invest in the information needed to convert uncertainty into risk. Some of these conditions are noted here. While several of them affect insolvency exposure directly as well as affecting it indirectly by encouraging disaster myopia, no attempt is made to evaluate all the factors influencing insolvency exposure.

Underinvestment in information is likely if decisionmakers believe they can reduce their exposure quickly and cheaply should shock probabilities suddenly rise. If the cost of maintaining flexibility is sufficiently low, there is little incentive to invest in information regarding the probability of a shock over the medium to long term or to set aside appropriate reserves.

Expectations of government assistance that would shield the firm from the full impact of a potential shock may also lead to underinvestment in information. Of course, expectations of government assistance can lead to excessive exposure even if decisionmakers have unbiased estimates of shock probabilities.

Compensation systems for managers that emphasize short-term performance can likewise discourage investment in information regarding low-frequency shocks. Decisionmakers will have little interest in determining and setting aside appropriate reserves if, by increasing the exposure of their firms, they can raise their own incomes while shielding themselves personally from the impact of a shock. The less frequent the shock and the higher the decisionmakers' job mobility, the greater will be the disparity between the exposure of decisionmakers and the exposure of their firms. Dysfunctional incentive systems may also play an independent role, just like expectations of government assistance. Even if shock probabilities are perceived without bias, the personal interests of decisionmakers may cause them to subject their firms to excessive insolvency exposure.

These factors are part of the process by which an institution becomes increasingly vulnerable to shocks that threaten its solvency. In this framework we examine international banking as an example of the phenomenon.

2   International Banking and Exposure to Transfer Shocks

International banks are subject to four basic kinds of shock: transfer shock, foreign-exchange shock, interest-rate shock, and funding shock.[4] A transfer

---

[4] We have avoided the traditional terms "transfer risk" and "liquidity risk" because in our framework the events to which these terms refer are governed more by uncertainty than by risk.

shock is a marked decline in the ability or willingness of foreign borrowers to convert their local currency into the currency in which interest and amortization payments are denominated. A foreign-exchange shock is an abrupt change in exchange rates that, depending on an institution's pre-existing foreign-exchange position, reduces its capital value and income. An interest-rate shock is an abrupt change in interest rates that, depending on the maturities of an institution's assets and liabilities, reduces its capital value and income. A funding shock is a sudden restriction of credit that jeopardizes an institution's ability to refinance maturing liabilities. Transfer shocks and foreign-exchange shocks are inherently international, while funding shocks have an important international component because many banks rely on the international interbank market. We will focus on transfer shocks and funding shocks, because they appear to pose the most substantial threats to the international financial system.

Exposure to Transfer Shocks

During the 1970s major international banks in all the industrialized countries substantially expanded their cross-border lending. By 1982 their exposures had become so large that the banks would suffer large, perhaps catastrophic, losses in the event of default by any one of several foreign borrowers. Table 1 illustrates this point for the nine major money-center banks in the United States. It lists all countries to which they had exposures (adjusted for external guarantees) exceeding 10 percent of capital in December 1982, just four months after the debt crisis erupted. Since these are averages for the nine banks, individual exposures must have been considerably higher in many cases. Among the ten largest U.S. banks, eight disclosed combined loan exposures to five countries experiencing debt-servicing difficulties—Argentina, Brazil, Chile, Mexico, and Yugoslavia—that were greater than 100 percent of equity. Three disclosed exposures to these troubled countries greater than 200 percent of equity (Bennett, 1983, p. D3).

Potential Hazards of Exposure to Transfer Shocks

Many countries have laws or regulations limiting bank exposures to individual borrowers, but these do not apply to countries. In the United States, for example, national banks are subject to a limit on the amount that they can lend to any one borrower, but under current interpretations each borrower within a foreign country is considered an independent entity if it has an independent means of repayment in its local currency and uses the loan proceeds in the "conduct of its business and for the purpose presented in the loan agreement."[5] (See Herring, 1985b, for an analysis of the case for lending limits.)

[5] Quoted by Ekin (1978). The Garn–St. Germain Act of 1982 increased the limits from 10 percent to 15, 20, or 25 percent, depending on circumstances.

TABLE 1
LARGEST EXPOSURES OF NINE U.S. MONEY-CENTER BANKS, ADJUSTED FOR GUARANTEES
(in percent of capital, December 1982)

	Exposure [a]	Exposure plus Contingent Claims [b]
Japan	73.3	84.7
United Kingdom	55.2	87.7
Brazil	48.8	52.1
Mexico	45.2	48.3
France	39.7	57.0
Canada	31.1	41.9
Germany, Federal Republic	26.3	34.8
South Korea	25.8	30.9
Belgium-Luxembourg	18.7	24.2
Italy	19.5	27.5
Spain	14.0	17.4
Philippines	13.1	15.6
Eastern Europe (total)	12.7	13.6
Australia	11.5	21.4
Hong Kong	11.0	17.7
Chile	11.0	12.3
Switzerland	10.2	18.2

[a] The numerator is the sum of cross-border, nonlocal currency claims on residents of the countries identified in the left-hand column, adjusted for external guarantees. The denominator is the total capital of the nine money-center banks, including equity, subordinated debentures, and provisions for loan losses, estimated to be $29.0 billion in December 1982. The nine banks are Bank of America, Bankers Trust, Chase Manhattan, Chemical Bank, Citibank, Continental Illinois, First National Bank of Chicago, Manufacturers Hanover, and Morgan Guaranty.

[b] Contingent claims, adjusted for external guarantees, are added to the numerator in the previous column.

SOURCE: Federal Financial Institutions Examination Council, *Statistical Release E.16*, 126 (June 1, 1983).

This interpretation of the lending limit ignores a fundamental distinction between domestic and foreign lending. Foreign borrowers that are independent entities in the sense of meeting the means and purposes tests are nevertheless linked in a way that independent domestic borrowers are not. Loans to foreign borrowers are subject to transfer shock—the possibility that the borrower will be unable to convert local currency into the currency in which the loan is denominated. Even when borrowed funds have been productively employed so that they increase the local-currency profits of a private borrower or the local-currency revenues of a governmental borrower, mismanagement of the economy as a whole can reduce net earnings of foreign exchange and interrupt debt-service payments. Politically motivated actions by the government can also block convertibility. Hence, the borrower's government is implicitly (if not directly) a party to each loan contract denominated in a foreign currency. In the worst case, debt service will stop on loans to *all* borrowers dependent on that government for foreign exchange.

High exposure to a specific country generates several related problems. The first and most obvious is the possibility of large losses on all outstanding loans to that country. If a sovereign borrower chooses to repudiate, losses may be very large, even total. Unless specific assets are pledged and are under the control of the lender, the legal remedies available to the lender may be very limited. Individual foreign borrowers that decide to repudiate may find it relatively easy to shield themselves from such legal remedies. Xenophobia may make it difficult for lenders to sue borrowers in local courts, and ways may even be found to avoid legal recourse in the third-party jurisdictions that are often specified in loan contracts. Even when legal recourse is available, bankruptcy costs are likely to be higher in a foreign default than in a domestic one. When the cause of default is an action by the borrower's government, legal recourse is often irrelevant, and the danger of a major write-down, even total repudiation, always lurks in the background.

The second problem is that heavy concentration puts excessive bargaining power in the hands of the borrower. A country's large indebtedness may place it in a position to gain by repudiating its debt, so that a threat of repudiation becomes a credible bargaining ploy. (See Eaton and Gersovitz, 1983, and Sachs and Cohen, 1982, for formal statements of the circumstances in which repudiation is optimal.) Indeed, a large borrower may *threaten* default, even when default can be avoided, as a way of extracting additional funds or more favorable terms. The threat of a default is potentially effective in international lending because the bank's usual defenses—the enforcement of restrictive convenants and the ability to attach the borrower's assets—are often useless when dealing with a sovereign power.

The third problem is that, even absent any tendency of a borrower to threaten a default, the borrower's payments difficulties may induce its creditors to increase their exposure even further so as to protect outstanding loans. A bank that initially set its exposure limit to a given country at x percent of capital may willingly allow its exposure to exceed that limit because the imminent possibility of losing x percent is more worrisome than the potential but more distant danger of an even higher exposure. This "quicksand" aspect—high exposure leading to even higher exposure through "bail-out" loans to borrowers in distress—can be contrasted to the banks' intended and often stated policy of keeping their options open so that they can respond flexibly to changed conditions.

Finally, once outstanding exposures become so large that a bank's unimpaired capital is smaller than the size of the bail-out loan required to protect its old loans, the bank's creditors and insurers are subject to grave moral hazard because they will share any future loss on the bail-out loan. Furthermore, the allocation of credit between domestic and foreign borrowers is seriously distorted. This may happen even before unimpaired capital falls below the size of the bail-out loan if the bank attempts to protect the book value of its claims as well as their true economic value. (See Herring, 1985b, for a formal analysis of the economics of bail-out lending.)

We believe that disaster myopia helps to explain why banks have subjected themselves to the hazards associated with heavy exposure to country risk. We will show that all the conditions conducive to disaster myopia, listed earlier, are present in international banking.

The Historical Pattern of Infrequent Shocks

An important factor contributing to disaster myopia is the infrequency of major shocks. The history of cross-border lending is characterized by long periods in which losses were low or nonexistent followed by a short period of calamitous losses. Foreign bonds marketed in the United States followed this pattern during the 1920s. No major default occurred from 1920 to 1930. Only two of some eight hundred individual issues suffered any interruption of debt service, and even those two continued to pay interest until 1929 and 1932, respectively. In 1937, however, 84 percent of bonds issued from 1920 to 1930 were in some degree of default (Mintz, 1951, pp. 29, 90, 91).

The history of lending to sovereigns tends to follow the same pattern. From the beginning, bankers have been aware that lending to a sovereign is hazardous because the sovereign's obligation to repay is unenforceable. In the fourteenth century, the three most important banks of the Middle Ages, headquartered in Florence but with branches spanning the known world—the Bardi, the Peruzzi, and the Acciajoli—were ruined when Edward III of England defaulted on a loan "equal to the value of a realm" (Bautier, 1971, p. 151).[6]

In the fifteenth century, the Medici were so keenly aware of the hazards of lending to sovereigns that strict prohibitions on such lending were included in the agreements incorporating their various subsidiaries. Nevertheless, the Medici began to make exceptions and eventually became heavily involved with Charles the Bold and Edward IV, the successor to the king who had bankrupted the Florentine banks. Defaults by these sovereign borrowers were partly responsible for the decline of the Medici bank. (For details, see de Roover, 1963.) A similar pattern is evident in the relationship between the Spanish Hapsburgs and the Fugger Bank, which became insolvent in the mid-seventeenth century after numerous moratoria and reschedulings of the sovereign's debts.

[6] Ehrenberg (1963, p. 50) reports that when these banks suspended payments, they "brought down with them in their fall most of the other Florentine banking houses."

9

Why did these banks lend to sovereigns? The temptations were great: the potential profits seemed large, and the sovereign, then as now, could give the banks access to substantial additional business. Moreover, most sovereigns were careful to repay their debts when those debts were small (often with the proceeds of new borrowing), making it all too easy to extrapolate favorable experience. As a sovereign's debts rose over time, however, the temptation to default must have risen correspondingly. Ehrenberg (1963, p. 131) reports that the Fugger Bank sustained a loss on its claims against the Hapsburgs equal to "the greater part of the Fugger's earnings in the course of a hundred years . . . ."

The Rewards of Heavy Exposure to Transfer Shocks

The rewards of heavy country concentration are returns generally higher than those obtainable on domestic lending, so long as no major shock occurs. This condition appears to have held in the 1970s. In a survey made by the Group of 30 (1982, p. 29), two-thirds of the banks reported that international lending was more profitable than domestic lending. Moreover, the loss rate on international loan portfolios appears to have been lower than on domestic portfolios. For example, Guenther (1981) reported that Citibank's losses from 1971 to 1980 averaged 0.29 percent of outstanding foreign loans compared with 0.70 percent for domestic loans.

While banks would undoubtedly prefer to diversify their holdings, their ability to do so is limited by the opportunities available. The point is illustrated by information given to us in early 1982 by a large Japanese bank. Its country lending quotas and its actual exposures, listed in order of magnitude, were as follows:

Quotas	Exposures
United States	Mexico
West Germany	Brazil
Canada	Italy
Australia	England
Switzerland	Canada

Only one country, Canada, is on both lists.

A country's net foreign borrowing can be viewed as filling a gap, the current-account deficit, that must equal the difference between domestic investment and savings plus the government's deficit. Therefore, most opportunities for net bank lending are in countries that run current-account deficits, as these are countries in which firms or the government will want to borrow. Indeed, the opportunities are limited to the subset of such countries in which the banks have confidence—those that can be expected to undertake

10

investments and follow macroeconomic policies that will enable them to service external debts.

Furthermore, the development of banking relationships with a country, which for a time allow a bank to earn excess returns, encourages concentration because of the substantial fixed costs involved. Once a bank has developed information sources and physical facilities in a country, additional loans can be made at a much lower marginal cost than in countries where customer relationships have not yet been established.

This tendency for customer relationships to produce heavy country concentrations is reinforced by the bargaining behavior of borrowers, who are likely to approach banks with a what-have-you-done-for-me-lately attitude.[7] Past loans are less important to the maintenance of a relationship than a willingness to make new loans. And aggressive country borrowers are likely to emphasize this point by making the continued placement of deposits and purchases of services for fees at least implicitly contingent on new lending.

Because there are negligible barriers to entry in the international loan market, returns above the competitive level tend to be eroded over time. Returns can be maintained in the face of such entry only if lenders (a) forgo the collection of an uncertainty premium for bearing the hazards of exposure to a major shock, and/or (b) allow their capital positions to decline or their exposure to funding shocks to rise.

Disaster Myopia and Poor Information

The attractive gross benefits of heavy country exposure in the short run do not translate into attractive net benefits in the long run if banks are subject to disaster myopia when they allow their exposures to increase.

During the 1970s, information was not readily available that would have limited the perceptual biases causing banks to be disaster-myopic about possible transfer shocks. Four decades had passed since the last episode of widespread country defaults, and most of the bankers who remembered it had faded from the scene. In any case, important structural changes in the world economy had occurred since the 1930s, such as the creation of the IMF, making it easy to discount the relevance of that experience.

In addition, the information that *was* available to estimate shock probabilities was very poor. Although information on debt-service obligations is critical for judging a borrower's ability to repay, banks routinely made loans without adequate data on the borrowing country's external debts. Information on international reserves, the balance of payments, and domestic economic activity was available only after a substantial lag, yet it, too, is essential for as-

---

[7] This shift in the balance of power between investor and borrower after investment has taken place is a principal theme in the literature on direct investment. See, for example, Eaton and Gersovitz (1983) or Vernon (1983).

11

sessing the effectiveness of a country's economic management. Banks seem to have had particular difficulty in evaluating covariances; they discounted the probability that several major borrowers would encounter payments difficulties at the same time.[8]

Edwards (1984) has examined the evolution of interest-rate spreads on syndicated loans for five Latin American countries that experienced payment difficulties in the 1980s. Using them to estimate the subjective probabilities of default for 1976-80, he found that the perceived probability rose significantly only for Venezuela. It declined for Argentina, Mexico, and Uruguay, and it rose only slightly for Brazil. Nonetheless, it seems likely that the true probability of a major transfer shock was, if anything, rising.

During this same period, interest-rate volatility increased markedly. Since most international lending was priced on a cost-plus basis—the interest rate was realigned with market rates every three to six months—the increased volatility of market interest rates led to increased volatility in debt-service payments. This volatility in debt-service payments was superimposed on a rising trend because of an increase in outstanding debt. Reliance on floating-rate loan contracts allowed banks to shift interest-rate shocks to borrowers. But when borrowers could not continue to sustain those shocks, this practice transformed interest-rate shocks into transfer shocks.

Exposure of Decisionmakers vs. Exposure of the Bank

During a period of expansion in profitable bank lending, the loan officers directly involved have increasing influence on the formulation of policy, and the influence of staff officers responsible for limiting exposure to shocks declines correspondingly. Profit-and-loss statements cover short periods, and the operating officers contribute directly to the firm's profits; the contribution of staff officers is less evident.

Banks make periodic allocations to reserves against losses, but these are typically based on losses already incurred or imminent, or losses that occur regularly and can therefore be expected with some statistical justification, such as those associated with consumer loans. No allowance is usually made for low-probability contingencies, as they are unlikely to generate losses within the current accounting period. This tendency is reinforced by tax laws that discourage the accumulation of reserves against low-probability hazards.

Since the compensation and power of loan officers are tied to current revenues from loan expansion, they have no incentive to invest in information that might counter disaster myopia. Their personal interest is in ignoring hazards that may not surface for a long time.[9] High job mobility reinforces this

[8] For a further discussion of the information problem, see Guttentag and Herring (1986a).

[9] A consultant on bank-executive compensation plans in the United States has told us that most large banks have incentive plans that tie compensation to annual performance. Incentive pay-

attitude, since the loan officer is likely to be in a different job, perhaps with a different bank, before trouble occurs.

Strategies for Avoiding Shocks: The Policy of
Revocable Commitments

Loan officers could not have dominated bank policy unless senior management had reason other than the loan officers' optimism for believing that any hazards inherent in current policies could be avoided or shifted. Avoidance is the objective of what we term the "policy of revocable commitments," the policy of keeping options open by taking positions that the bank believes can be reversed at short notice.

In the case of country-loan exposure, this policy is implemented mainly by limiting loan maturities.[10] As noted in Citibank's 1981 Annual Report (p. 26), ". . . country risk from foreign currency lending is reduced as the length of the obligation decreases, since shorter maturities permit adjustments in exposure as balance of payments or political conditions change." The presumption is that a possible contingency can be perceived on the horizon before it occurs, so that the perceptive banker will have time to avoid it. This presumption weakens the motivation to invest in information that would help to formulate shock probabilities and might counter disaster myopia.

Unfortunately, the strategy of dealing with uncertainty by making revocable commitments usually does not work, because it is subject to the fallacy of composition. Short maturities may protect a single creditor that has superior information and can shift exposure to other banks before they perceive the danger.[11] But the strategy cannot protect all creditors, because debtor countries are seldom in a position to reduce their total debt significantly in a short period. Certainly, all creditors will not be able to shift exposure if the bank with superior information has perceived the situation correctly. The most likely result of an attempt by better-informed banks to shift exposure onto other banks is a crisis of confidence in the borrowing country's ability to pay. In that case, the effective maturity of all creditors' claims against that country is extended indefinitely.

Implicit Government Support

If international banks expect to be protected by governments against the full consequences of any shock, they will be encouraged to disregard the proba-

---

ments to high-ranking officers are tied to the overall performance of the bank, while those to lower-ranking officers are usually tied to the performance of divisions or departments.

[10] The maturities on international loans are limited for several other reasons as well (Guttentag and Herring, 1983b).

[11] This is one reason why it is often difficult for banks to develop a common bargaining strategy when a debt crisis occurs. Since they have failed to shed their exposure at the time of the crisis,

bility of shocks. Such expectations may lead them to underinvest in information that might counter disaster myopia or to ignore relevant evidence. They justifiably assume that the chances of getting such protection are better if they "herd," keeping insolvency exposure, especially capital ratios and exposures to individual countries, roughly in line with those of their peers. Herding converts any major problem into a problem for the whole banking system, raising the specter of a general financial crisis if the government fails to assist the banks.

Competition

International banking markets tend to be competitive. It is estimated, for example, that at least a thousand banks were active in the international interbank market in 1980, and other banks are always waiting in the wings. From 1973 to 1980, an annual average of sixty-six financial institutions entered the Euroloan market for the first time (see Page and Rogers, 1982, pp. 61-62).

Competition interacts with tendencies toward disaster myopia in two related ways. First, competitive markets make it impossible for lenders that are not disaster myopic to price loans as if there were a finite probability of a major shock when banks that *are* disaster myopic price them as if that probability were zero. Competition from new entrants appears to have been a contributing factor to the narrowing of spreads in the 1970s. A Group of 30 survey (1982, p. 39) of the sources of "pressures on spreads" indicates that 70 percent of respondents rated as very important "aggressive pricing by lenders seeking to enter new markets." Second, if international banks are apparently earning returns above the competitive level (disregarding the need for reserves against future shocks), they will encourage new entry by equally myopic banks, which will tend to erode those returns. Banks can protect target rates of return on capital for a time by allowing their capital positions to decline (or, as discussed below, their funding exposure to rise). Disaster-myopic decision-makers within banks (or suboptimizers who are not concerned with long-run consequences) can rationalize such actions in terms of the need to maintain target returns in the face of shrinking margins, and in terms of similar actions by other banks. But as their capital and liquidity positions become marketplace norms for pricing decisions, returns above the competitive level can be maintained only by further adjustments. Hence, disaster myopia facilitates a competitively driven process that increases the insolvency exposure of international banks along several dimensions.

The process may be terminated by a major shock that jolts perceptions and reveals that uncertainty premiums have been grossly deficient or exposures

---

all are sensitive to the issue of *changes* in exposure as the result of a debt restructuring. No bank is willing to increase its own exposure so that others can reduce theirs.

excessive. (A preferable outcome is for supervision to constrain the tendency toward rising vulnerability before a major shock occurs, but such supervision is very difficult, as we shall see in section 4.) Evidence that shock probabilities have risen is unlikely, by itself, to have a significant effect.

The Persistence of Disaster Myopia

The reluctance of decisionmakers to react to evidence that shock probabilities have risen once their exposures have become very high is a reflection of "cognitive dissonance," a psychological mechanism that protects the decisionmaker's self-esteem when new information casts doubt on the wisdom of past decisions. Cognitive dissonance is likely to be resolved by ignoring the new information, rejecting it, or accommodating it by changing other beliefs in ways that serve to justify past decisions.

Evidence of cognitive dissonance does not necessarily indicate that erroneous prior decisions regarding exposure were caused by disaster myopia. Well-founded decisions may go awry. But we would expect decisionmakers who have developed the information sources, analytical procedures, and habits of inquiry that counter disaster myopia to change their views more readily when new information challenges them.

While there is no particular reason to believe that bankers as a group are more subject to cognitive dissonance than, say, university professors or civil servants, bankers appear to have been afflicted by cognitive dissonance during the period just before the eruption of the debt crisis in August 1982. Otherwise, it is difficult to explain why banks were so slow to react to signs of impending debt-servicing difficulties.[12] A recent IMF report (Brau et al., 1983, p. 5) notes: "Of the non-oil developing countries that either have restructured or were in the process of restructuring their bank debt between 1978 and the third quarter of 1983, all experienced a period of very rapid increase in international bank loans prior to the development of debt service difficulties." Although some of the increase in banks' exposure was due to borrowers that drew on previously established commitments, much of the increase was attributable to new short-term lending just before the crisis. This lending even financed capital flight by residents of the borrowing countries who had lost confidence in the policies of their own governments. That fact

---

[12] Strains in the debt-servicing ability of major borrowing countries were apparent well before the August 1982 crisis. In May 1980, for example, we noted that "the actual probabilities of a credit shock in the Eurocurrency market appear to have increased over time, especially in recent years. The key factors are the increasing financial vulnerability of several debtor countries and the increasing concentration of claims on these countries in the portfolios of several major banks" (Guttentag and Herring, 1980). In June 1981, we took the affirmative in a debate with Jack Guenther of Citibank on the issue "Is a Global Debt Crisis Looming?" (ABA, 1981, and Guenther, 1981).

should have been evident to the major international banks experiencing a rise in their deposit liabilities to residents of those countries.

3 International Banking and Exposure to Funding Shocks

Lest the analysis above be viewed as 20-20 hindsight regarding a shock that has already occurred, we turn next to a type of exposure that has not yet generated a crisis: exposure to a funding shock. We follow the same outline as before but exclude factors associated with disaster myopia that are common to exposure to both transfer shocks and funding shocks.

Exposure to Funding Shocks

Since 1961, when Citibank began to issue negotiable CDs and efficient dealer markets in those CDs were established, major banks have become increasingly dependent on liability management rather than asset management to regulate their liquidity positions.[13] They depend on their ability to borrow (as opposed to their ability to liquidate assets) to meet unexpected as well as anticipated cash needs.[14]

Some measures of this dependence are shown in Table 2 for March 31, 1984, shortly before the managers and shareholders of Continental Illinois National Bank paid the ultimate price of illiquidity. At that time, more than three-quarters of Continental's total liabilities were "volatile liabilities." Volatile liabilities are short-term and interest-rate sensitive. Presumably, they are also sensitive to shifts of confidence in the borrowing bank. Deducting short-term assets from volatile liabilities and relating the difference to long-term assets provides a measure of "volatile-liability dependence." Continental used volatile liabilities to finance 82.5 percent of its long-term assets (see column 1 of Table 2). While Continental's ratio was the highest of any major

[13] "Liability management" is used here in the narrow sense of dependence on the ability to borrow to meet unexpected cash needs. The term is often used in a broader sense to mean the practice of issuing marketable liabilities to meet asset targets, as opposed to "passively accepting whatever deposit liabilities the public desires to hold and then distributing those funds among potential borrowers" (Silber, 1977, p. 1). These two uses of the term "liability management" are not usually differentiated, because major U.S. banks developed both practices together. As banks replaced government securities with claims on the private sector and the growth of demand deposits slackened, it became necessary to support further asset growth by issuing interest-bearing liabilities. By making these liabilities negotiable and encouraging the development of dealer markets in them, banks could also manage their liabilities to meet short-term liquidity requirements. Yet financing asset growth by issuing marketable liabilities does not necessarily imply the use of liability management for liquidity purposes. Banks could still protect themselves against unanticipated cash needs by holding short-term liquid assets.

[14] In a partial reversal of this trend, banks have recently attempted to enhance the liquidity of their assets by devising marketable loans. For an analysis of such efforts, see Guttentag and Herring (1986b).

TABLE 2

MEASURE OF FUNDING-SHOCK EXPOSURE FOR SELECTED U.S. BANKS

(in percent, March 31, 1984)

Bank	Volatile-Liability Dependence (1)	Deposits in Foreign Offices to Total Volatile Liabilities (2)	Volatile Liabilities to Banks to Total Volatile Liabilities (3)	Volatile Liabilities to Foreign Banks to Total Volatile Liabilities (4)
Continental Illinois	82.5	58.7	49.9	29.8
Morgan Guaranty	81.6	61.4	29.0	14.2
1st National Chicago	77.0	56.7	29.6	21.2
Mfrs. Hanover	72.5	61.1	35.1	21.3
Citibank	72.2	71.1	30.1	17.4
Chase Manhattan	71.1	71.6	23.7	14.4
Bankers Trust	70.3	55.0	37.5	17.7
Chemical	57.2	52.2	34.3	11.7
Bank of America	46.5	60.1	24.7	18.0
All banks over $10 billion assets	61.4	50.9	NA	NA
All banks $3-$10 billion assets	31.1	25.2	NA	NA
All banks $1-$3 billion assets	18.7	10.5	NA	NA

NOTE: Volatile liabilities consist of all time deposits over $100,000, foreign-office deposits, federal funds purchased and securities sold under repurchase agreements, interest-bearing demand notes issued to the U.S. Treasury, and other liabilities for borrowed money. Volatile-liability dependence is total volatile liabilities less "temporary investments" (interest-bearing balances due from banks, federal funds sold and securities purchased under agreement to resell, trading-account assets, and investment securities with remaining maturities of one year or less), divided by the sum of net loans and lease-financing receivables and debt securities either repriceable or with remaining maturities of more than one year. Volatile liabilities to banks exclude transaction accounts (which are not included in total volatile liabilities). Liabilities to foreign banks include deposits of U.S. branches and agencies of foreign banks and exclude deposits of foreign branches of U.S. banks. Federal-funds purchases and securities sold under repurchase agreement are assumed to be liabilities to U.S. banks.

SOURCES: Figures for individual banks are from *Uniform Bank Performance Report* (cols. 1 and 2) and *Reports of Condition* (cols. 3 and 4), while figures for the two bank groups are from the *Peer Group Report*. All reports are published by the Federal Financial Institutions Examination Council and are dated as of March 31, 1984.

bank at that time, it was only marginally higher than that of several other money-center banks.

More than half of the volatile liabilities of major U.S. banks in 1984 were deposits purchased through the foreign offices of U.S. banks (column 2), and from a fourth to a half were liabilities to other banks (column 3). For six of the nine banks, volatile liabilities to foreign banks exceeded volatile liabilities to U.S. banks (compare columns 3 and 4). Dependence on foreign banks is, in fact, understated by column 4, which assumes that purchases of federal funds and sales of securities under repurchase agreements are entirely domestic. (A foreign-domestic breakdown is not available.)

The major money-center banks in the United States are thus heavily dependent on their ability to raise large amounts in short periods by borrowing, and a large proportion of their borrowing sources are foreign, especially foreign banks. In this regard, the money-center banks are outliers among other U.S. banks, as indicated by the comparable measures for other large U.S. banks shown in the last two rows of Table 2.

Exposure to funding shocks is an international banking problem in several respects. First, in the U.S. case at least, major international banks are much more heavily exposed than other banks. (Data on exposures of foreign banks are not readily available.) Second, excessive exposures to funding shocks (indeed, exposures to all shocks) are particularly difficult to constrain by regulation in a competitive international environment, as we argue below. Finally, one important market on which these banks depend is the international interbank market. The increasing depth and breadth of this market that accompanied the spread of cross-border banking encouraged reliance on liability management, although such reliance began much earlier for U.S. banks, with the development of domestic markets for claims on banks.[15]

The Growth of the International Interbank Market

Cross-border lending involves lending to banks as well as to governments and other nonbank borrowers. Many cross-border loans to nonbanks are facilitated by and lead to cross-border interbank relationships that involve deposit holdings. Frequently, moreover, banks lending to foreign nonbanks find it efficient to obtain the needed currency by borrowing from banks in third countries that have more cost-effective ways of obtaining that currency. In addition, when banks undertake cross-border flows to exploit international differences in interest rates and loan opportunities, they often prefer to lend to other banks because, for a variety of reasons, they have more confidence in them than in foreign nonbanks. Finally, once interbank markets become well organized, banks find it advantageous to use them for adjusting their funding,

[15] For an analysis of how the development of a market for claims on banks influences liability management, see Guttentag and Herring (1985c).

18

interest-rate, and foreign-exchange exposures, as well as for other purposes.[16]

The result is that cross-border interbank claims account for a large proportion of all cross-border claims. For banks in Canada, Europe, and Japan, interbank claims were 70 percent of total foreign-currency claims in 1981, while for external loans denominated in the domestic currency of the lending bank, the proportion was 54 percent (BIS, 1983, p. 18). For U.S. banks, whose cross-border claims are largely in U.S. dollars, about 70 percent of the total are interbank (Clarke, 1983). Excluding claims against the banks' own offices abroad, the U.S. figure drops to about 50 percent (see *Federal Reserve Bulletins*, Table 3.19).

The international interbank market grew at a remarkably rapid rate during the 1970s, although reliable data are available only since 1975. Between 1975 and 1981, cross-border interbank claims of banks in Canada, Europe, and Japan (in both domestic and foreign currencies) rose from $246 billion to $777 billion (BIS, 1983, p. 23).[17] Market observers suggest that there were no more than two hundred banks in the market in 1973 but well over a thousand in 1982. According to Pierre Jaans (1979, p. 26), Commissioner of Banks in Luxembourg, there has been a downward trend in the size of banks that are able to operate in international financial markets. Since the Latin American debt crisis, however, the number of banks has shrunk somewhat, with many Latin American banks shut out of the market.

It might be thought that claims on banks held by other banks would not be as volatile as claims held by nonbanks, because of the greater knowledge and sophistication of bank creditors, but this is not the case. For one thing, bank claims often are large relative to the creditor bank's capital. For example, an investigation of claims against Continental Illinois National Bank, just before the run, found that 66 banks had exposures to Continental Illinois in excess of their capital and another 113 had exposures between 50 and 100 percent of their capital.[18]

In addition, the information that banks have about other banks is often meager, sometimes of questionable relevance, and often out-of-date by the time it is available (see Guttentag and Herring, 1985c, and BIS, 1983). Even in the United States, where banks disclose more information than anywhere else, it is not possible to determine the exposure of a bank to other individual banks. (Lack of detailed information is dangerous because of potential spillover effects; the funding problem of bank A can spill over to bank B if the mar-

---

[16] For discussions of the various uses of the international interbank market, see Herring (1985a) and Guttentag and Herring (1985c).

[17] There is a major break in the series between 1977 and 1978. BIS (1983) contains a useful discussion of problems involved in defining the market and measuring its size.

[18] Memorandum to Chairman Isaac of FDIC from Robert V. Shumway, dated June 20, 1984. This memorandum is shown in an appendix to H.R. Committee on Banking, Finance and Urban Affairs (1984).

ket suspects that B is heavily exposed to A.) Information regarding foreign banks is even poorer. The level of disclosure to the market (as opposed to disclosure to regulatory authorities) is far lower abroad than in the United States, and published balance sheets in many countries are designed to conceal rather than reveal. The widespread practice of maintaining hidden reserves is designed to stabilize reported earnings and avoid large charge-offs against reported net worth in the event that the bank suffers substantial losses.

In general, creditor banks rely less on considered judgments regarding a borrowing bank's solvency than on the borrower's general reputation, which is subject to reevaluation on short notice in response to "bad news." Banks thus rely on the strategy of revocable commitments as much or more in lending to other banks as in lending to countries.

Potential Hazards of Exposure to Funding Shocks

The more a bank depends on liability management, the more vulnerable it is to a bank-specific funding shock associated with a decline in the market's confidence in that bank's solvency. Its survival rests on its ability to place new liabilities at least equal to the amount by which maturing liabilities exceed maturing and readily salable assets. Net cash outflow within a specific future period, appropriately scaled and projected on the assumption of no new borrowing, is a measure of the bank's exposure to a funding shock (see Guttentag and Herring, 1986c). The greater this exposure, the greater is the danger that a shock to creditors' confidence in the bank's solvency will generate a run by holders of maturing claims from which the bank will not be able to recover. Faced with an unwillingness by some depositors to roll over maturing claims, a heavily exposed bank may be forced to offer higher interest rates, which may be interpreted by others as a signal that the bank is in trouble, leading to a further curtailment of supply. If the bank turns to its lender of last resort (LLR) for more than routine amounts, that also may be interpreted by the market as an adverse signal, and all other sources may dry up. (The reasons will be discussed later.) If the amounts required from the LLR become very large, that agency may feel obliged to take control of the bank.

While data on daily borrowing requirements are not publicly available—indeed, the amounts involved are very erratic—we have seen enough daily funding sheets of major banks to be impressed by the size of those requirements. It would not be unusual, for example, for the amount of LLR assistance required by a major bank to run from $5 to $20 billion in a matter of days if all other sources fell away.

In contrast, the liquidity position of a bank practicing asset management is much more secure. To be sure, it may be adversely affected by a major shock that increases the perceived default risk on assets held for purposes of liquid-

20

ity adjustment. But this risk can be minimized by holding obligations of the government or assets guaranteed by the government.[19] Even if its assets are private obligations, the bank can protect itself by diversifying. In contrast, the bank practicing liability management must protect itself against a shock that affects the market's perception of the default risk on the bank's own liabilities. This is more difficult, since adverse perceptions of a given bank are likely to spread through all the markets in which that bank operates.[20]

To the degree that a bank practicing liability management depends on access to an LLR when other sources desert it, the bank's exposure to a funding shock rises with the total amount it may have to borrow in a short period. The larger this amount, the larger is the implied social subsidy extended by the LLR and the greater is the pressure on the LLR to terminate it quickly.

The Continental Illinois episode is a case in point. Continental suffered its first shock following the failure of the Penn Square Bank on July 6, 1982. Continental had purchased from Penn Square large participations in energy loans of questionable quality. In the weeks following the collapse of Penn Square, Continental experienced a severe funding problem as large amounts of domestically held CDs and federal funds were withdrawn. To replace them, Continental turned to the international interbank market. (Other banks suffering domestic funding problems, like the First Pennsylvania Bank in 1980, had also been able to borrow in the international money market long after domestic sources had dried up.) By replacing domestic CDs, federal funds, and other liabilities with increased borrowings from foreign banks, Continental avoided massive borrowings from the Federal Reserve. The maturities of the interbank loans were evidently quite short, however, and funding costs were higher than before.

Over the subsequent months, Continental's funding problems gradually stabilized, but the bank remained highly vulnerable to another funding shock because of the large volume of short-term liabilities to foreign banks. Furthermore, the bank's loan-portfolio problems turned out to extend beyond its Penn Square participations. The volume of nonperforming loans gradually rose. On May 8, 1984, a rumor erupted that the bank was facing imminent bankruptcy. Confidence evaporated with alarming rapidity, especially among

[19] Of course, exchange controls or variations in exchange rates could make the obligations of one government an unsatisfactory store of liquidity for cash needs denominated in the currency of another government.

[20] This does not imply that diversification of liabilities is useless. For one thing, diversification of funding sources protects against shocks affecting the sources of funds, as opposed to shocks affecting the borrowing bank. In addition, some liability holders are likely to be more sensitive to "bad news" than others. Sensitivity, moreover, is likely to be greater the larger the amounts held by the creditor. These considerations are discussed at greater length in Guttentag and Herring (1986c).

foreign banks, and Continental was quickly forced to borrow $3.7 billion from the Federal Reserve, the amount later rising above $7 billion.[21]

On May 17, just nine days after the first rumors had appeared in the market, the FDIC, in conjunction with the Federal Reserve and the Comptroller of the Currency, took the unprecedented step of explicitly guaranteeing all creditors' claims on the bank. The guarantee was part of a comprehensive assistance program, but it did not stem the run, and the Federal Reserve and FDIC were finally forced to assume *de facto* control of the bank.

The Historical Pattern of Infrequent Shocks

It is well understood that when the solvency of a bank is called seriously into question, it will suffer liquidity problems from uninsured creditors who become unwilling to roll over their claims. Within the last decade, this has happened to Franklin National, First Pennsylvania, SeaFirst, and most recently to Continental Illinois. Yet these episodes did not significantly reduce the heavy reliance of other money-center banks on liability management (at least until just before the run on Continental Illinois in March 1984), because there were no serious spillover effects to other banks. With the exception noted below, the last period of contagious transmission of liquidity shocks from one bank to another was the 1930s, and the financial structure has changed substantially since then.

The only case where the failure of one bank led to a contagious loss of confidence that adversely affected the liquidity positions of other banks was the failure of Bankhaus ID Herstatt, a relatively small German bank, in June 1974. The failure of Herstatt threatened the stability of the international banking system, but it was due to the particular way the bank was closed, which is unlikely to be repeated, and to certain structural weaknesses in the international interbank market that have since largely been repaired (see Guttentag and Herring, 1985c).

While the Latin American debt crisis reduced the total number of banks that could borrow in the international interbank market, again there was no significant contagion, nor were there illiquidity-induced failures.[22] Hence, the impact on liquidity-management practices was negligible. The dependence of major banks on volatile liabilities declined very modestly after 1981, but it is not clear how much of the decline, if any, was due to the debt crisis.[23]

[21] See Continental Illinois Corporation (1984, p. 11).

[22] For a more extensive discussion, see Guttentag and Herring (1985c).

[23] Comparisons of dependence on volatile liabilities before and after the debt crisis are influenced by the coincidental authorization granted to depository institutions under the Garn–St. Germain Act to offer money-market deposit accounts (MMDAs). Since MMDAs are classified as core rather than volatile liabilities, their rapid growth during this period tended to reduce dependence on volatile liabilities. It is thus no accident that the two major banks whose dependence on volatile liabilities fell the most (Bank of America and Chemical) were also the two with the largest growth in MMDAs, reflecting their extensive branch systems.

The smaller banks ($1-$10 billion in assets), much less dependent on volatile liabilities to begin with, reduced their dependence by about one-third, whereas the largest banks reduced it by less than one-tenth. Among the nine major money-center banks, the largest reductions were made by the two (Chemical and Bank of America) that were the least dependent in 1981. In their dependence on volatile liabilities, the major banks had therefore become more extreme outliers in 1984 than they were in 1981.

Thus, despite the increasing number of failures of banks of significant size in recent years and a debt crisis of major proportions, a contagious loss of confidence has not occurred. Without such a shock, there has been no significant change in the operating assumption of major banks that the positive benefits from liability management outweigh the dangers.

The Rewards of Heavy Exposure to Funding Shocks

Obviously, major banks would not expose themselves to funding shocks if it were not profitable. Liability management is more economical than asset management as a way of meeting precautionary liquidity needs when the return on liquid assets is significantly below that on illiquid assets and banks can fill their portfolios with the latter.[24] The interest foregone by holding liquid assets for long periods, until they are used to meet liquidity needs, exceeds the cost to banks of issuing their own liabilities, even at a rate above the liquid-asset rate, because the liabilities will be outstanding for a much shorter period. This requires, of course, that there be a well-developed market for the banks' own liabilities. Experience suggests, however, that when banks find it profitable to use liability management, markets in bank claims arise to accommodate them.[25]

The availability of a "lender of first resort" (such as the Federal Reserve's short-term adjustment credit) provides a cheap way to meet very-short-run needs of the "white noise" type. It thus encourages liability management by reducing the frequency of unexpected cash drains for which provision must be made either by holding liquid assets or by husbanding the power to borrow in the private market. And the availability of a reliable lender of last resort reduces the fear that a major shock to confidence in a bank will lead to a run that will cause the failure of the bank practicing liability management.

A second source of profits from liability management is derived from "play-

---

[24] If banks need to hold liquid assets as an investment, the rate differential between liquid and illiquid assets is not a determinant of the relative cost of practicing asset management as opposed to liability management. During the years immediately following World War II, banks still held large amounts of government securities as an investment, because the level of demand for private loans had not yet forced a complete replacement of one by the other. Asset management was a costless way to provide for liquidity. This was particularly the case prior to 1951, because the prices of government securities were pegged by the Federal Reserve.

[25] The most dramatic illustration was Citibank's decision to issue negotiable CDs in 1961, which was made jointly with dealers who had agreed to make a market in them.

ing the yield curve." The very short end of the yield curve is generally up-ward-sloping, but most of those who borrow for one or a few days use the funds for longer-term purposes, subjecting themselves to a funding shock. It is not surprising that the major international banks are active as very-short-term borrowers, because they are the best equipped of all the borrowers in the marketplace (except perhaps governments) to assume this exposure.

As noted earlier, however, the ease of new entry into international banking markets tends to erode above-competitive market returns derived from as-suming heavy exposure to funding shocks. Eventually, such exposure be-comes necessary for all major banks in order to earn a competitive return, while all banks have become exposed to the danger that a major shock to con-fidence in their solvency will sharply limit their ability to place their liabili-ties.

Disaster Myopia and Poor Information

As with country exposure, insufficient information is available to establish the probability of a funding shock. Since a funding shock is likely to follow a shock to a bank's actual or perceived solvency from *any* source, including a country default, the information problem is inherently intractable. A funding shock stemming from a contagious loss of confidence originating with the failure of *another* bank has not occurred since the 1930s, and there is no basis for as-sessing its probability. Thus, conditions are favorable for disaster myopia.

Yet the probability of a major shock to confidence in the solvency of any single bank has been growing as a result of the reduced capital positions of major banks from the levels of ten to fifteen years ago, of the foreign-debt cri-sis, and of problems in the energy, agriculture, and real-estate sectors that have raised questions about the true value of loan portfolios. Weaker capital positions increase the probability of contagion in two ways. First, a loss from any type of shock is more likely to jeopardize a bank's solvency; second, the failure of one bank is more likely to call into question the solvency of other banks that may have similar exposures, or claims on the failed bank.

Moreover, in the United States the ability of the lender of last resort to re-store market confidence in a solvent bank that is subject to a run has been eroded by recent practices of the Federal Reserve. In theory, an LLR lends only to solvent banks (see Guttentag and Herring, 1983a). Hence, an LLR's decision to extend credit to a bank from which other lenders are running should constitute a signal to the market that the bank is sound. By dampening adverse expectations regarding the bank's condition, the LLR should reas-sure creditors, and the amount of credit required of the LLR should be very small.

In recent years, however, the Federal Reserve has sustained insolvent banks pending an orderly disposition by the FDIC. For example, the Federal

24

Reserve made massive advances to keep Franklin National, First Pennsylvania, SeaFirst, and Continental Illinois operating until a final disposition could be made. As a result, markets now regard large credit extensions by the Federal Reserve as an indicator of likely insolvency rather than the reverse. A bank known to be borrowing more than routine amounts from the central bank thus runs the grave risk that it will quickly find it can borrow *only* from the central bank. A money-center bank in this position would require such massive assistance that the central bank would have little choice but to assume *de facto* control.

Bank managers appear to understand this. After the first shock to market confidence in its solvency in the wake of the collapse of Penn Square in June 1982, Continental Illinois made a policy decision that it would avoid borrowing from the Federal Reserve if it possibly could. It succeeded in doing so, although the short-term cost in terms of higher interest rates and slower growth was very high. When the second shock hit in May 1984 and Continental Illinois could no longer avoid borrowing heavily from the Federal Reserve, news of the borrowing further undermined confidence in the bank.

Implicit Government Support

We noted in connection with exposure to transfer shocks that a perception that the government would provide assistance in the event of a major shock affecting many banks probably encouraged disaster myopia, even though the amount of government support actually provided was modest (see Guttentag and Herring, 1985b). In the case of exposure to funding shocks, expectations of government assistance should not necessarily encourage disaster myopia, because a major bank can have a liquidity crisis without affecting other banks. Furthermore, the Continental Illinois episode clearly showed that both the stockholders and the management of such a bank could lose heavily.

But it is also true that the Continental Illinois case was merely the most recent illustration of the fact that governments usually *do* protect bank creditors, justifying the perception that claims against major banks are supported by implicit government guarantees. This perception facilitates the efficient functioning of the worldwide interbank market. It also permits major banks that are believed to be covered by such guarantees to fund themselves more cheaply and encourages them to rely more heavily on liability management.[26]

Yet implicit guarantees are not sufficient to prevent a run because they cannot be certain. Some ambiguity is inevitable if the guarantee is not explicit. Lack of complete confidence in the guarantee, along with the ready availabil-

---

[26] Capital requirements in several important jurisdictions, including Belgium, France, Germany, and Switzerland, lend official support to the notion that interbank claims are safer than claims on nonbanks. In evaluating adequacy of capital, these countries require banks to hold more capital against claims on nonbanks than against claims on banks.

ity of comparable claims against trouble-free banks, provide an incentive to run; maturing liabilities provide the opportunity.

The importance of explicit guarantees is highlighted by the Continental Illinois case. Just nine days after the run started, the U.S. authorities took the unprecedented step of explicitly guaranteeing "all depositors and other general creditors of the bank."[27] The guarantee was part of a comprehensive financial-assistance program that included a capital infusion of $2 billion ($1.5 billion from the FDIC and $0.5 billion from a group of commercial banks), an increase in unsecured credit lines from other banks to $5.5 billion, and an assurance that the Federal Reserve was prepared to meet any extraordinary liquidity requirements of the bank during this period.

Despite these actions, the run did not stop. When we asked banks why they still refused to lend to Continental Illinois, we were told that the FDIC guarantee did not have sufficient explicit legal safeguards. Thus, implicit guarantees may have the pernicious effect of encouraging banks to place deposits with other banks on the basis of cursory credit evaluations, while offering no real protection against a funding shock when a borrowing bank gets into trouble.

In summary, we cannot demonstrate that the probability of a contagious liquidity shock exceeds some uncomfortable level, let alone that such a shock will occur. We do know, however, that exposure to such shocks has increased markedly over the last two decades. This reflects the increasing dependence of banks on markets in which they can sell their liabilities to meet their liquidity needs (including the highly volatile interbank market), the inability of major banks to borrow substantial amounts from the Federal Reserve without undermining confidence in their own solvency, and compelling evidence that there has been an increase in the probability of shocks to confidence in the solvency of individual banks. We also know that this increase in exposure to liquidity shocks has occurred under conditions conducive to disaster myopia: liability management has been profitable in the absence of shocks; there has not been an episode of contagious transmission of liquidity shocks since the 1930s; and there is no reliable objective method of assessing the probability of such a shock.

It is very unlikely that there will be significant changes in current liquidity-management practices without a major liquidity shock. As with exposure to transfer shocks, market pressures make it extremely difficult for any one bank to adopt more prudent policies when the absence of such a shock bolsters the disaster myopia of others.

---

[27] Joint Press Release by the Comptroller of the Currency, the Federal Deposit Insurance Corporation, and the Federal Reserve Board, May 17, 1984.

4 Supervising International Banks

The Need for Prudential Regulation

Can government supervision do what the private market cannot? The underlying premise of prudential bank supervision is that banks, unless constrained, will sometimes assume insolvency exposure that is excessive from a social point of view. One reason is that creditors of banks may not require default premiums that sufficiently penalize banks for the insolvency risk they assume. Creditors may lack information about a bank's exposure to shocks. Moreover, creditors may be explicitly insured and therefore unconcerned about a bank's condition, or they may believe themselves to be implicitly insured because their bank is considered too large and important to be allowed to fail.

A second reason why banks may assume excessive insolvency exposure is that banks consider the potential impact of failure on their stockholders and management but not the secondary repercussions on other banks and on confidence in the financial system as a whole. Yet it is generally believed that the secondary repercussions from the failure of a very large bank can be extremely important. (Indeed, this is why creditors not explicitly insured often feel that they are insured *de facto* if they have claims against a major bank.)

In addition, a bank with depleted capital has a special incentive to assume large insolvency exposures, because the benefits will accrue to shareholders and management while the downside costs will be borne at least in part by creditors or insurers. Such banks we describe as being in "go-for-broke mode."

This essay has identified another factor underlying excessive insolvency exposure that is probably more important than any other in contributing to the vulnerability of the banking system (as distinct from the vulnerability of individual banks). This is the tendency of banks to underestimate or ignore low-probability shocks that could have major adverse effects. We have attributed this to a general human tendency to be myopic about low-probability shocks, as well as to accounting systems that encourage short planning horizons, competitive markets that force banks to ignore such shocks in pricing credit, and other factors.

The Uncertainty Quandary

Unfortunately, when shock probabilities are governed by uncertainty, there is no objective way, even in principle, to determine *ex ante* that a bank is excessively exposed. This poses a major supervisory quandary. The bank-supervisory process as it has evolved over the decades is not well designed to deal with exposure to major shocks of unknown probability. Instead, the primary thrust of supervision has been to assess the current condition of a bank. Even the computerized "early warning systems" recently adopted by supervisors in the United States are designed to catch early indications of emerging weakness associated with developments already in process (see Flannery and Guttentag, 1980).

It is very difficult for supervisors to deal with a bank in good condition that would be seriously damaged by a shock of unknown probability, since reasonable persons could easily disagree about the probability of such an eventuality. The difficulty comes at three levels. The first is defining exposure to the hazard. Exposures to transfer, funding, interest-rate, and foreign-exchange shocks can all be defined in a variety of defensible ways. Supervisors are loathe to insist on one definition of exposure, although occasionally they have done so. The Federal agencies in the United States, for example, have now defined exposure to transfer shocks for purposes of public disclosure (see Guttentag and Herring, 1985a). But they have not defined exposure to any of the other shocks listed above.

The second problem is more difficult. Even when exposure can be well defined, supervisory authorities do not believe that they are competent or have the legal authority to establish exposure limits. The supervisory approach in connection with exposure to transfer shocks probably represents the practical limit to the exercise of their authority in the absence of an explicit legislative directive. The approach involves a uniform definition of exposure by the agencies, which is then used to assure that (a) banks know what their exposures are relative to the aggregate exposure of other banks; (b) banks have adequate internal-management systems for making exposure decisions; and (c) bank directors are informed of exposures exceeding specified levels defined by the supervisory authorities.

This "measure and confront" approach to shock exposure has the merit of forcing banks to face the issue. To the degree that disaster myopia is encouraged by inattention and poor communications among operating officers, senior management, and directors, such procedures are a useful corrective.[28] They may also constrain suboptimization by decisionmakers whose personal time horizons are very short. However, the forces described earlier that lead to excessive exposure are very powerful.

There is a third difficulty. During periods when optimism prevails, bank supervisors using traditional approaches to assessing the banks' condition are likely to share the banks' disaster myopia. The measure-and-confront approach to constraining exposure to transfer shocks was adopted in the United States only *after* exposures had reached very high levels.[29]

[28] For a discussion of the problem of institutionalizing measures to combat disaster myopia within the firm, see Guttentag and Herring (1986c).

[29] It is interesting that although the savings and loan industry in the United States was brought

28

This is not meant as a counsel of despair. Supervisors are in a stronger position to resist disaster myopia than banks, provided they organize the supervisory process around the need to constrain banks from assuming excessive exposure. This calls, among other things, for explicit procedures to identify shocks having nontrivial probabilities and for various types of exposure limits comparable to the traditional limits on the portion of a bank's capital that can be loaned to a single entity. In a forthcoming study, we will develop this theme in some detail.

Capital Requirements

Rather than set exposure limits, however, supervisors have been forcing banks to hold more capital in order to increase their ability to absorb any kind of shock. In many European countries, capital requirements are imposed in a mechanical, quantitative fashion. In Switzerland, for example, required capital is calculated for each bank based on the composition of that bank's assets and liabilities. In the United States, capital requirements used to be more judgmentally based, but this approach failed to stem the erosion of capital positions that began decades ago, and the United States has shifted to a more formal system of capital requirements. Title IX of the International Lending Supervision Act of 1983 required the bank-regulatory agencies to set "minimum levels of capital" for each bank and to relate this minimum to country-risk exposure (see Guttentag and Herring, 1985a). The agencies have since established minimum capital-asset ratios for all banks and in 1986 proposed a new system of risk-adjusted capital ratios.

Capital requirements have a number of problems. One is that banks often find ways to comply that do not actually increase their ability to bear losses from shocks. These evasions are made possible by capital requirements formulated in terms of the book value of capital, whereas the true ability to bear losses is measured by the market value of capital.[30] Thus, in 1985, in response to the new requirements imposed on U.S. banks, many banks sold their head-

---

to the brink of insolvency by a severe interest-rate shock during 1978-81, the Federal supervisory agency with responsibility for their safety and soundness (the Federal Home Loan Bank Board) did not begin to evolve a measure-and-confront approach to exposure to interest-rate risk until 1984.

[30] The market value of capital or "economic net worth" is the difference between the market value of *all* the bank's assets less the present value of the bank's liabilities. The measure of the bank's assets should be comprehensive, including not only tangible assets and financial claims that appear on the balance sheet, but also the present value of options such as lines of credit, acceptances, and forward contracts, and the present value of intangible assets such as the bank's charter, customer relationships, and the expertise of the bank's managers. For further discussion of economic net worth and biases in using book net worth to monitor economic net worth, see Guttentag and Herring (1982).

quarters office buildings in order to realize profits that increased capital ratios based on book values of capital but not ratios based on market values.

Even if capital requirements did force banks to hold more capital than they would otherwise have held, there is a second problem. If banks are free to increase their exposures, the greater ability to bear shocks may be neutralized by greater shock exposures, and insolvency exposure may not decline (see Santomero and Watson, 1977, and Herring and Vankudre, 1986). This is particularly likely when capital ratios are set with regard to recorded balance-sheet exposures but banks are free to increase their exposure to shocks through off–balance-sheet transactions.

The seemingly obvious remedy is to tie capital requirements to exposures, including off–balance-sheet exposures. Indeed, as noted above, legislation in 1983 required the U.S. bank-regulatory agencies to tie capital requirements to country-risk exposures, and in principle this approach could be extended to other types of shock exposure. While this approach imposes an arbitrary relationship between required capital increments and exposure, this difficulty is unavoidable. It applies as well to establishing absolute risk-exposure limits, which is the only feasible regulatory alternative.

The more important problem is that regulators are likely to recognize a particular type of exposure as sufficiently dangerous to justify requiring additional capital only *after* a shock occurs. Thus, incremental capital requirements against country exposures have been adopted by bank regulators only since the debt crisis, and for the most part they have been applied only to the countries already experiencing debt-servicing problems. In contrast, as far as we know, no attempts have been made to tie capital requirements to funding exposure. Tying capital requirements to exposures *ex ante* (before the shocks occur) rather than *ex post* encounters all the difficulties inherent in traditional regulatory mindsets and procedures referred to earlier.

A third problem with capital requirements is that supervisors cannot impose on U.S. banks capital standards that are far out of line with those imposed on foreign banks without crippling their competitiveness.[31] Cooperation among national supervisory authorities has advanced in recent years, most notably in facilitating exchanges of information on problem banks and in agreement on the principle of consolidation in assessing bank soundness. So far, however, little progress has been made in harmonizing differing regulatory provisions, including capital requirements.[32]

---

[31] The Group of 30 study (1982, p. 5) reports that "A majority of American banks (and a minority of European and other banks) complain of burdensome regulations which could be modified or dropped without impairing prudential control"; and "American bankers feel more strongly than any other group that regulation by their authorities puts them at a disadvantage in international competition."

[32] The paper on the supervision of banks' off–balance-sheet exposures published in 1986 by the

Finally, international banks may be able to defeat capital requirements by overleveraging their foreign subsidiaries. This issue is very closely related to a broader issue, the responsibility of international banks for their subsidiaries.

Overleveraging and Responsibility for Subsidiaries

When a bank extends its operations through control over a subsidiary that is legally a separate corporate entity, it may feel justified in increasing the insolvency exposure of the consolidated firm because it views its liability as limited. Subsidiaries with limited liability may give the parent bank a convenient mechanism for reducing its consolidated capital position if it is predisposed to do so. The parent bank decreases the capital of the subsidiary while assuming a "moral responsibility" to the subsidiary's creditors, thus allowing the subsidiary to borrow on the parent's name.

This practice may be dangerous if creditors of subsidiaries are subject to disaster myopia. A parent may choose to let a troubled subsidiary fail if a bail-out does not serve the parent's business interest at the time—perhaps because a bail-out would severely weaken the parent. This is a reasonable inference from the fact that banks typically accept a moral but not a legal responsibility for their subsidiaries, although they *could* accept a legal responsibility. If a subsidiary gets into trouble and the parent decides against assuming liability, unwary creditors of the subsidiary may be in for an unpleasant surprise. Another possibility is that the parent is in for an unpleasant surprise when it finds that liability is thrust upon it.[33]

Uncertainty regarding the responsibility of parents for subsidiaries exists in domestic markets, but the probability that the parent will attempt to evade responsibility in a crisis is much greater if the subsidiary is in another country. Political and regulatory pressures to assume responsibility are stronger domestically, as the subsidiary is the responsibility of a domestic regulator rather than a foreign regulator. Furthermore, bank ownership of foreign subsidiaries is more frequently only partial, diluting the responsibility of any one owner.

Excessive leveraging can be countered by consolidating subsidiaries with their parents when assessing exposure to shocks and applying prudential standards such as capital requirements or exposure limits. The Standing

---

Committee on Banking Regulations and Supervisory Practices is a first step toward harmonizing capital requirements in the key industrial countries.

[33] If creditors of a failed subsidiary can demonstrate that they were led to believe that dealing with the subsidiary was like dealing with the shareholder bank itself, the bank may be compelled to satisfy the subsidiary's creditors. This is the rule in the United States (for further details, see Posner, 1976), but the United States may not be the legal jurisdiction in which a specific issue is considered.

Committee on Banking Regulation and Supervisory Practices, composed of representatives from the Group of 10 plus Switzerland and Luxembourg, has recently adopted the principle of consolidated supervision in a revision of the "Concordat," an agreement regarding international supervisory cooperation (Committee on Banking Regulations and Supervisory Practices, 1983).

Whether consolidation succeeds in constraining the tendency of international banks to leverage excessively through subsidiaries depends on the effectiveness with which it can be applied. This is a major issue that cannot be fully developed here, but three important problems should be noted. First, consolidation for supervisory purposes does not eliminate the *incentive* to overleverage unless the regulatory authorities require their banks to assume full legal liability for their foreign subsidiaries. None of them has done so, at least in part because national authorities do not wish to encumber their own banks (and themselves) with responsibility for foreign banks. Second, consolidation is difficult to implement when the subsidiary is a nonbank (since capital standards vary by industry), and especially difficult when ownership of the nonbank entity is only partial.[34] Third, even if consolidation could be perfectly applied, competitive considerations limit the enforcement of prudential standards on the consolidated entity when different standards are imposed by other supervisors.

In summary, bank supervision traditionally has given the least emphasis to the most important problem affecting the insolvency exposure of international banks, namely, excessive exposure to major shocks of low but unknown probability. Concerns about shock exposures and attempts to induce banks to measure and confront them have come only after major shocks have occurred, which is precisely when supervisory-imposed constraints are not needed. Instead of confronting the need for *ex ante* exposure limits, the thrust of supervision has been to increase the ability of banks to absorb shocks by requiring them to hold more capital. For a variety of reasons, this approach is very unlikely to be effective.

5   Concluding Comment

The evaluation of policies to deal with bank exposure to insolvency must confront a fatalistic rationale for ignoring it: the world is full of low-probability hazards carrying very high potential costs for which no bank can prepare, such as nuclear war or an economic depression. This is true, but it misses the

---

[34] The Luxembourg firm Banco Ambrosiano Holdings SA was a partially owned subsidiary of Banco Ambrosiano of Italy that was not subject to consolidated supervision by the Italian authorities. Even if the Italian authorities had been inclined to supervise, they could not have done so because Luxembourg's secrecy laws deprived them of information on the subsidiary. The firm was not supervised by Luxembourg's banking commissioner either, since it was not a bank.

point. Fatalism is inappropriate when there are means available to avoid a hazard or to mitigate its impact significantly. International banks can control their exposure to some kinds of shock even though they are powerless to limit their exposure to other catastrophic events.

This essay demonstrates the difficulties of constraining tendencies toward excessive insolvency exposure before the occurrence of a shock when shock probabilities are perceived to be low. The forces pressing toward overexposure are powerful both within and outside each bank. They affect bank supervisors as well. And the international scope of bank operations limits the range of preventive measures. Our view is that strategic planning to control insolvency exposure should be an explicit and integral part of the overall planning of each bank, and that the entire thrust of bank supervision needs to be reconsidered along the same lines. These are topics on our research agenda.

References

ABA Banking Journal editors, "Is a Global Debt Crisis Looming? 'Yes' Say Two Wharton Professors," *ABA Banking Journal* (June 1981), p. 48.

Bank for International Settlements, "The International Interbank Market: A Descriptive Study," *BIS Economic Papers*, No. 8, July 1983.

Bautier, Robert-Henri, *The Economic Development of Medieval Europe*, New York, Harcourt Brace Jovanovich, 1971.

Bennett, Robert A., "Top Bank's Third World Loans Detailed," *New York Times* (Mar. 18, 1983), p. D3.

Brau, E., and R. W. Williams with P. M. Keller and M. Nowak, "Recent Multilateral Debt Restructurings with Official and Bank Creditors," *Occasional Paper 25*, International Monetary Fund, December 1983.

Clarke, Stephen V. O., *American Banks in the International Interbank Market*, New York, Salomon Brothers Center for the Study of Financial Institutions, Monograph 1983-4, 1983).

Committee on Banking Regulations and Supervisory Practices, "Principles for the Supervision of Banks' Foreign Establishments," press release, Basel, May 1983.

————, "The Management of Banks' Off-Balance-Sheet Exposures: A Supervisory Perspective," Basel, 1986, mimeographed.

Continental Illinois Corporation, *Prospectus*, Aug. 24, 1984.

de Roover, Raymond, *The Rise and Decline of the Medici Bank, 1397-1494*, Cambridge, Mass., Harvard University Press, 1963.

Eaton, John, and Mark Gersovitz, "Country Risk: Economic Aspects," in R. J. Herring, ed., *Managing International Risk*, New York, Cambridge University Press, 1983, pp. 75-108.

Edwards, Sebastian, "LDC Foreign Borrowing and Default Risk: An Empirical Investigation, 1976-80," *American Economic Review*, 74 (September 1984), pp. 726-734.

Ehrenberg, R., *Capital and Finance in the Age of the Renaissance: A Study of the Fuggers and Their Connections*, New York, Augustus M. Kelly, 1963.

Ekin, Thomas C., Address to the Syndicated Eurocredit Conference, June 14, 1978.

Flannery, Mark, and Jack Guttentag, "Problem Banks: Identification, Examination and Supervision," in *State and Federal Regulation of Commercial Banks*, Task Force on State and Federal Regulation of Commercial Banks directed by Leonard Lapidus, FDIC, 1980.

Group of 30, *How Bankers See the World Financial Market*, A Survey by the Office of the Group of 30, 1982.

Guenther, Jack D., "Is a Global Debt Crisis Looming? 'No' Says a Citibank Senior V.P." *ABA Banking Journal* (June 1981), pp. 49-50, 105.

Guttentag, Jack M., and Richard Herring, "Financial Disorder and Eurocurrency

Markets," in *Bank Structure and Competition*, Federal Reserve Bank of Chicago, May 1-2, 1980.

———, "The Insolvency of Financial Institutions: Assessment and Regulatory Disposition," in Paul Wachtel, ed., *Crisis in the Economic and Financial Structure*, Lexington, Mass., Heath, 1982.

———, *The Lender-of-Last-Resort Function in an International Context*, Essays in International Finance No. 151, Princeton, N.J., Princeton University, International Finance Section, May 1983a.

———, "What Happens When Countries Cannot Pay Their Bank Loans? The Renegotiation Process," *Journal of Comparative Business and Capital Market Law*, 5 (1983b), pp. 209-231.

———, "Credit Rationing and Financial Disorder," *Journal of Finance*, 39 (December 1984), pp. 1359-1382.

———, *The Current Crisis in International Lending*, Studies in International Economics, Washington, D.C., The Brookings Institution, 1985a.

———, "Commercial Bank Lending to Developing Countries: From Overlending to Underlending to Structural Reform," in J. Cuddington and G. Smith, eds., *International Borrowing and Lending: What Have We Learned from Theory and Practice?* Washington, D.C., World Bank, 1985b.

———, "Funding Risk in the International Interbank Market," in W. J. Ethier and Richard C. Marston, eds., *International Financial Markets and Capital Movements: A Symposium in Honor of Arthur I. Bloomfield*, Essays in International Finance No. 157, Princeton, N.J., Princeton University, International Finance Section, September 1985c, pp. 19-32.

———, "Disclosure Policy and International Banking," *Journal of Banking and Finance*, 10 (1986a), pp. 1-23.

———, "Financial Innovations to Stabilize Credit Flows to Developing Countries," *Studies in Banking and Finance*, 3 (forthcoming 1986b).

———, "Strategic Planning by International Banks to Cope with Uncertainty," in P. Savona and G. Sutija, eds., *Strategic Planning and International Banking*, London, Macmillan, 1986c.

Herring, Richard J., "The Interbank Market," in P. Savona and G. Sutija, eds., *Eurodollars and International Banking*, London, Macmillan, 1985a, pp. 111-121.

———, "The Economics of Bailout Lending," Philadelphia, Wharton Program in International Finance and Banking, April 1985b, mimeographed.

Herring, Richard J., and Prashant Vankudre, "Growth Opportunities and Risk-Taking by Insured Intermediaries," January 1986, mimeographed.

H.R. Committee on Banking, Finance and Urban Affairs, *Continental Illinois National Bank Failure and Its Potential Impact on Correspondent Banks*, Staff Report to the Subcommittee on Financial Institutions Supervision, Regulation and Insurance, Oct. 4, 1984.

Jaans, Pierre, "Measuring Capital and Liquidity Adequacy for International Banking Business," in *International Conference of Banking Supervisors*, London, July 5-6, 1979.

Kunreuther, Howard, R. Ginsberg, L. Miller, P. Sagi, P. Slovic, B. Borkin, and N. Katz, *Disaster Insurance Protection: Public Policy Lessons*, New York, Wiley, 1978.

Lucas, Robert, "Understanding Business Cycles," in K. Brunner and A. M. Meltzer, eds., *Stabilization of the Domestic and International Economy*, Amsterdam, North-Holland, 1977, p. 729.

Mintz, Ilse, *Deterioration in the Quality of Foreign Bonds Issued in the United States, 1920-30*, New York, National Bureau of Economic Research, 1951.

Page, Diane, and Walter D. Rogers, "Trends in Eurocurrency Credit Participation, 1972-80," in *Risks in International Bank Lending*, New York, Group of 30, 1982.

Posner, Richard A., "The Rights of Creditors of Affiliated Corporations," *University of Chicago Law Review*, 43 (Spring 1976), pp. 499-526.

Sachs, Jeffrey, and Daniel Cohen, *LDC Borrowing with Default Risk*, NBER Working Paper No. 925, July 1982.

Santomero, Anthony M., and Ronald A. Watson, "Determining an Optimal Capital Standard for the Banking Industry," *Journal of Finance*, 32 (September 1977), pp. 1267-1282.

Silber, William L., *Commercial Bank Liability Management*, New York, Association of Reserve City Bankers, 1977.

Simon, Herbert A., "Rationality as Process and as Product of Thought," *American Economic Review*, 68 (May 1978), pp. 1-16.

Slovic, P., B. Fischoff, S. Liechtenstein, B. Corrigan, and B. Combs, "Preference for Insuring against Probable Small Losses: Insurance Implications," *Journal of Risk and Insurance*, 45 (June 1977), pp. 237-258.

Tversky, Amos, and Daniel Kahneman, "Availability: A Heuristic for Judging Frequency and Probability," in D. Kahneman, P. Slovic, and A. Tversky, eds., *Judgment under Uncertainty: Heuristics and Biases*, New York, Cambridge University Press, 1982, pp. 163-178.

Vernon, Ray, "Organizational and Institutional Responses to International Risk," in R. J. Herring, ed., *Managing International Risk*, New York, Cambridge University Press, 1983, pp. 191-216.

PUBLICATIONS OF THE
INTERNATIONAL FINANCE SECTION

Notice to Contributors

The International Finance Section publishes at irregular intervals papers in four series: ESSAYS IN INTERNATIONAL FINANCE, PRINCETON STUDIES IN INTERNATIONAL FINANCE, SPECIAL PAPERS IN INTERNATIONAL ECONOMICS, and REPRINTS IN INTERNATIONAL FINANCE. ESSAYS and STUDIES are confined to subjects in international finance. SPECIAL PAPERS are surveys of the literature suitable for courses in colleges and universities.

An ESSAY should be a lucid exposition of a theme, accessible not only to the professional economist but to other interested readers. It should therefore avoid technical terms, should eschew mathematics and statistical tables (except when essential for an understanding of the text), and should rarely have footnotes.

A STUDY or SPECIAL PAPER may be more technical. It may include statistics and algebra and may have many footnotes. STUDIES and SPECIAL PAPERS may also be longer than ESSAYS; indeed, these two series are meant to accommodate manuscripts too long for journal articles and too short for books.

To facilitate prompt evaluation, please submit three copies of your manuscript. Retain one for your files. The manuscript should be typed on one side of 8½ by 11 strong white paper. All material should be double-spaced—text, excerpts, footnotes, tables, references, and figure legends. For more complete guidance, prospective contributors should send for the Section's style guide before preparing their manuscripts.

How to Obtain Publications

A mailing list is maintained for free distribution of all new publications to college, university, and public libraries and nongovernmental, nonprofit research institutions.

Individuals and organizations not qualifying for free distribution can obtain ESSAYS and REPRINTS as issued and announcements of new STUDIES and SPECIAL PAPERS by paying a fee of $12 (within U.S.) or $15 (outside U.S.) to cover the period January 1 through December 31, 1986. Alternatively, for $30 they can receive all publications automatically—SPECIAL PAPERS and STUDIES as well as ESSAYS and REPRINTS.

ESSAYS and REPRINTS can also be ordered from the Section at $4.50 per copy, and STUDIES and SPECIAL PAPERS at $6.50. Payment MUST be included with the order and MUST be made in U.S. dollars. PLEASE INCLUDE $1 FOR POSTAGE AND HANDLING. (These charges are waived on orders from persons or organizations in countries whose foreign-exchange regulations prohibit such remittances.) For airmail delivery outside U.S., Canada, and Mexico, there is an additional charge of $1.

All manuscripts, correspondence, and orders should be addressed to:
International Finance Section
Department of Economics, Dickinson Hall
Princeton University
Princeton, New Jersey 08544

Subscribers should notify the Section promptly of a change of address, giving the old address as well as the new one.

List of Recent Publications

Some earlier issues are still in print. Write the Section for information.

ESSAYS IN INTERNATIONAL FINANCE

140. Pieter Korteweg, *Exchange-Rate Policy, Monetary Policy, and Real Exchange-Rate Variability*. (Dec. 1980)
141. Bela Balassa, *The Process of Industrial Development and Alternative Development Strategies*. (Dec. 1980)
142. Benjamin J. Cohen, *The European Monetary System: An Outsider's View*. (June 1981)
143. Marina v. N. Whitman, *International Trade and Investment: Two Perspectives*. (July 1981)
144. Sidney Dell, *On Being Grandmotherly: The Evolution of IMF Conditionality*. (Oct. 1981)
145. Ronald I. McKinnon and Donald J. Mathieson, *How to Manage a Repressed Economy*. (Dec. 1981)
*146. Bahram Nowzad, *The IMF and Its Critics*. (Dec. 1981)
147. Edmar Lisboa Bacha and Carlos F. Díaz Alejandro, *International Financial Intermediation: A Long and Tropical View*. (May 1982)
148. Alan A. Rabin and Leland B. Yeager, *Monetary Approaches to the Balance of Payments and Exchange Rates*. (Nov. 1982)
149. C. Fred Bergsten, Rudiger Dornbusch, Jacob A. Frenkel, Steven W. Kohlhagen, Luigi Spaventa, and Thomas D. Willett, *From Rambouillet to Versailles: A Symposium*. (Dec. 1982)
150. Robert E. Baldwin, *The Inefficacy of Trade Policy*. (Dec. 1982)
151. Jack Guttentag and Richard Herring, *The Lender-of-Last Resort Function in an International Context*. (May 1983)
152. G. K. Helleiner, *The IMF and Africa in the 1980s*. (July 1983)
153. Rachel McCulloch, *Unexpected Real Consequences of Floating Exchange Rates*. (Aug. 1983)
154. Robert M. Dunn, Jr., *The Many Disappointments of Floating Exchange Rates*. (Dec. 1983)
155. Stephen Marris, *Managing the World Economy: Will We Ever Learn?* (Oct. 1984)
156. Sebastian Edwards, *The Order of Liberalization of the External Sector in Developing Countries*. (Dec. 1984)
157. Wilfred J. Ethier and Richard C. Marston, eds., with Kindleberger, Guttentag and Herring, Wallich, Henderson, and Hinshaw, *International Financial Markets and Capital Movements: A Symposium in Honor of Arthur I. Bloomfield*. (Sept. 1985)
158. Charles E. Dumas, *The Effects of Government Deficits: A Comparative Analysis of Crowding Out*. (Oct. 1985)
159. Jeffrey A. Frankel, *Six Possible Meanings of "Overvaluation": The 1981-85 Dollar*. (Dec. 1985)

160. Stanley W. Black, *Learning from Adversity: Policy Responses to Two Oil Shocks*. (Dec. 1985)
161. Alexis Rieffel, *The Role of the Paris Club in Managing Debt Problems*. (Dec. 1985)
162. Stephen E. Haynes, Michael M. Hutchison, and Raymond F. Mikesell, *Japanese Financial Policies and the U.S. Trade Deficit*. (April 1986)
163. Arminio Fraga, *German Reparations and Brazilian Debt: A Comparative Study*. (July 1986)
164. Jack M. Guttentag and Richard J. Herring, *Disaster Myopia in International Banking*. (Sept. 1986)

PRINCETON STUDIES IN INTERNATIONAL FINANCE

45. Ian M. Drummond, *London, Washington, and the Management of the Franc, 1936-39*. (Nov. 1979)
46. Susan Howson, *Sterling's Managed Float: The Operations of the Exchange Equalisation Account, 1932-39*. (Nov. 1980)
47. Jonathan Eaton and Mark Gersovitz, *Poor Country Borrowing in Private Financial Markets and the Repudiation Issue*. (June 1981)
48. Barry J. Eichengreen, *Sterling and the Tariff, 1929-32*. (Sept. 1981)
49. Peter Bernholz, *Flexible Exchange Rates in Historical Perspective*. (July 1982)
50. Victor Argy, *Exchange-Rate Management in Theory and Practice*. (Oct. 1982)
51. Paul Wonnacott, *U.S. Intervention in the Exchange Market for DM, 1977-80*. (Dec. 1982)
52. Irving B. Kravis and Robert E. Lipsey, *Toward an Explanation of National Price Levels*. (Nov. 1983)
53. Avraham Ben-Bassat, *Reserve-Currency Diversification and the Substitution Account*. (March 1984)
*54. Jeffrey Sachs, *Theoretical Issues in International Borrowing*. (July 1984)
55. Marsha R. Shelburn, *Rules for Regulating Intervention under a Managed Float*. (Dec. 1984)
56. Paul De Grauwe, Marc Janssens, and Hilde Leliaert, *Real-Exchange-Rate Variability from 1920 to 1926 and 1973 to 1982*. (Sept. 1985)

SPECIAL PAPERS IN INTERNATIONAL ECONOMICS

10. Richard E. Caves, *International Trade, International Investment, and Imperfect Markets*. (Nov. 1974)
*11. Edward Tower and Thomas D. Willett, *The Theory of Optimum Currency Areas and Exchange-Rate Flexibility*. (May 1976)
*12. Ronald W. Jones, *"Two-ness" in Trade Theory: Costs and Benefits*. (April 1977)
13. Louka T. Katseli-Papaefstratiou, *The Reemergence of the Purchasing Power Parity Doctrine in the 1970s*. (Dec. 1979)
*14. Morris Goldstein, *Have Flexible Exchange Rates Handicapped Macroeconomic Policy?* (June 1980)
15. Gene M. Grossman and J. David Richardson, *Strategic Trade Policy: A Survey of Issues and Early Analysis*. (April 1985)

20. William H. Branson, *Asset Markets and Relative Prices in Exchange Rate Determination*. [Reprinted from *Sozialwissenschaftliche Annalen*, Vol. 1, 1977.] (June 1980)
21. Peter B. Kenen, *The Analytics of a Substitution Account*. [Reprinted from *Banca Nazionale del Lavoro Quarterly Review*, No. 139 (Dec. 1981).] (Dec. 1981)
22. Jorge Braga de Macedo, *Exchange Rate Behavior with Currency Inconvertibility*. [Reprinted from *Journal of International Economics*, 12 (Feb. 1982).] (Sept. 1982)
23. Peter B. Kenen, *Use of the SDR to Supplement or Substitute for Other Means of Finance*. [Reprinted from George M. von Furstenberg, ed., *International Money and Credit: The Policy Roles*, Washington, IMF, 1983, Chap. 7.] (Dec. 1983)
24. Peter B. Kenen, *Forward Rates, Interest Rates, and Expectations under Alternative Exchange Rate Regimes*. [Reprinted from *Economic Record*, 61 (September 1985).] (June 1986)

ISBN 0-88165-071-4